Lily Is Leaving:

Poems by Leslie A. Fried

Cirque Press

Copyright © 2021 Leslie A. Fried

All rights reserved. No part of this publication may be reproduced, distributed or transmitted in any form or by any means, including photocopying, recording, or other electronic or mechanical methods, without the prior written permission of the publisher, except in the case of brief quotations embodied in critical reviews and certain other noncommercial uses permitted by copyright law.

Published by

Cirque Press

CIRQUE PRESS

Sandra Kleven — Michael Burwell

3157 Bettles Bay Loop

Anchorage, AK 99515

Print ISBN: 9798589712766

cirquejournal@gmail.com

www.cirquejournal.com

Illustrations and Design Concept by Leslie Fried

Book Design by Carly Egli

For my mother Lillian

Contents

I

Apart — 10

Lily is Leaving — 13
Existential Texas — 14
Afterwards — 15
Poem for My Mother's Yahrzeit — 17
I Think of Jesse Leaving — 18

II

Laws of Attraction — 20

Dune Shack — 23
Nightdress — 25
Intimate Dinner — 26
Red Dress — 28
[You lay there] — 29
Lilikoi — 30

III

Nightscapes — 32

Border Town — 35
The Bride in the Lime Pit — 36
This Way and That — 38
Station Café — 39
Special Collections — 40

IV

Love and Pain 42

Terminal Moraine 45
Writer whose work still moves me to tears 48
Thrill 49
Aching in the Lowlands 50
I Saw Two Crows 51
Travail 53

V

Shipwreck and Resurrection 58

[When I was crazy] 61
Seward First Winter 62
Living After Winter 64
The Boys Outside 65
White Frozen Postcard 66
In Spring 68

VI

How and Why 70

Levee 73
Death of the Fish Lizard 74
Why Children 75
Slick 76
Son I wish 77
Love you forever, lady who gave me life 78

VII

History Lessons	80
My Alphabet Begins with Y	83
Playhouse in a Vacant Lot	84
One and Only Love	85
A Boy with Lizard Eyes	86
In Ostende	87
Opera	88
Dancing from Warsaw to Vilna in Black and White	90

Apart

Lily is Leaving

the way that summers end
softly, in fading light
the spicy scent of leaves smoldering
and distant cries from the beach

slipping away
she becomes a frail version of herself
each part unfamiliar to the others
separate in their suffering she is noble
dispensing potions from the bed
and incantations "water, water" or
"where is Leslie"
curling her fingers through mine

Lily is leaving
sailing back to white shoulders
bazillion bird wing flutters
muscle of universe pumping slow time
now the particulars become the general
cashmere in winter
the veiled cloche the Kaddish cup
Mother Earth as seen from space
everything and nothing.

Existential Texas

It's winter it rains
I read a book take a train go east from Seattle
a year ago today someone in my house died
three weeks from a shipwreck in a bar
two weeks past coffee and flowers
one week all night shivering drunk-assed
two days after sex.

on the train my shadow is my letter of introduction
a tin medallion
byss and abyss
the business of being
tis most certain thou shalt be free from trouble and want
the last time, he sighed and whispered my name.

the train shush-shush-shushes through a flat cracked game board
a copper colored caddy slinks along the access road
I close my eyes I see winter, a proud beast
see limbs disconnected under that sheet
as sooty careless clouds drift across Texas
like God's ink blotter.

invitation to a farewell dinner.

Afterwards

I remember your wish
to "drop my ashes over Puget Sound
and make sure Hugo's the pilot"
Hugo hasn't flown in years
wears flip flops, shades
and speaks a very sexy Franglais
I pay for his license

the day arrives the airport is deserted
does it close for last rites
and where is the audience of
ex-wives and lovers, mother, brother, kids, step-kids
bar buddies and fellow poets
there is only me and one troubled son

after a desperate run down the tarmac
and a thundering lift-off
we are swallowed into azure haze
the pint-sized plane flipping about
like a tormented beach ball
but you, your ash body calm in sleep
nestle gently against my side
in paper packets scented with rose petals

I slide open the tiny window
and with a beating of wings, in rush
ancient worlds of mourning widows
hair flying upward feet pointing down
women of a singular beauty
with eyes of shell and lapis

Afterwards

they call me Habibi, lead me down teeming streets
to the pyre where birds fly up
and tell me to shake the ash
beat my breast and wish you well
as you fade into a circle of light, the collective dead

Hugo lights a cigarette
I don't have a speech only mutter
"thank-you"
I'm imagining your new home
on the sea floor
in the bellies of wolf fish
along with the sea urchins, cockles and green crabs.

Poem for My Mother's Yahrzeit

The marshland is slow to wake
under a wooly cloud cover
my train to Talkeetna
bumps and waddles
through fat golden grass

Turnagain
in shadow to the right
Knik River
snaking to the left
skating silver over eyelids
and then sun's radiance
morning bath

yellowlegs, plover and dabbling ducks
scurry, swoop and dive
trumpeter swan!
reddening leaves ride magnificently
down to winter filling my heart
this first year without you.

I Think of Jesse Leaving

There was his bedroll, frail sheet
woolen blanket not good for rain
and I asked,
because you're going,
could we lie down together
look at me
I would look at you
rearrange the pieces.

Listen baby
there are three points of connection to me now
in this room when I'm gone
think of them as blow-holes
fire tubes, light tunnels
stand just so
and I will get it.

I thought of the ride out to Georgetown
knock on the door
stand in the spot
face the three points and call
please   come   back
and I knew that he wouldn't
with my eyes closed.

The last time I saw Jesse was in a dream
carefully, a waltz of one
woody giants dripping
blood in the forest
laughter of Raven
tolling through the fog
the time for departure.

Shoes, hat, two songs, a poem
placed in a circle
around like a farewell hug
too tight to linger
"I understand," I yelled
"I'm not mad"
as the forest drew back
and all the bending, twisting and breaking remained.

Laws of Attraction

Dune Shack

We are:
shacking up again in the dune shack
great ball of sun pasted to the window
puts things in a new light

from outside it's a well-built box
you said holds cows and hens
and other domesticated creatures
for me a poet's lair sex on stormy nights
desolate gull shriek mornings of
hobo coffee or hot jasmine brought from the city

plenty big back then for two
you know the universe in an eyebrow
everything had its place
pot of water warming in the sun
soft-bodied worm tidal flat sea
strata of worn sheet to skin and hair
sole to rattan

summoned here by you to talk I think
of Brewster Road and remember going back
to the house bought by Father in 1958
with enough room for a wife and five children
how had we all fit?

hot throated asshole I cannot forgive you
the nest of mice babies you fed to the cat
this still stands all that was us,
who gets it you should have it the kids just the summer

Dune Shack

your voice is receding burrowing the last word
into sand leaving a vague impression susceptible to wind
and myself at the window like the seated woman of Boeotia
long strong fingers and no face draped in carved stone.

Nightdress

Oh butterfly
in your nightdress
hiding in the bedclothes
waiting to be ravished
I will ravish you!
your peony lips
sensual, yes
and sly, the eyelashes
at my throat
your way of speaking
in the dark.

Oh butterfly
nightdress
so modest
in white
with you I am solemn
and ferocious
love me
in all my disarray.

Intimate Dinner

In the mailbox I find
a small white envelope
buried under ads
for discount tires and slab bacon.

I imagine you
marking the words carefully
Invitation to an Intimate Dinner
Room 43, Airport Way South.

I imagine you
marking the words carefully
with your Waterman Ideal No. 52
in quirky penmanship.

I see a small square table
covered in butcher paper
folded and taped
and a mattress made up
with clean sheets and a pretty afghan.

A small square table
covered in butcher paper
a trout in a bent pan on the hotplate
its crispy tail hanging over
and dead eye waxy grey.

Trout sizzling in a bent pan
dandelions on the sill
pulled from a patch outside
bread from the market on a plate
with butter pats.

Dandelions on the sill
throbbing with portent
a girl running down radiant
her Indian shawl billowing
as I run up.

A girl runs down radiant
as I run up for love
the mattress remade
with clean sheets
and the pretty afghan.

I accept with sharpened pencil
a Derwent Graphic 2B
Intimate Dinner, Room 43,
Airport Way South.

Red Dress

I see red
I want to wear it to a bar
be a long-stemmed invitation
runaway umbrella
more
much more
than a fabulous something

I see red I want to take it off
you and your life
shape-shifter
enter me like a pebble
you can't make it right

I see red
on her as night perfume not me
that's why I mess around
with this poem.

[You lay there]

You lay there
pasha with languorous eyes
a password was spoken
in the quiet
and my limbs softened
they began to wrap themselves
around you
and squeeze for life

It was really the same old thing
draped in a new magnificence
lit with a new lamp
through a blessed haze
of forgetfulness.

Lilikoi

Please, don't be like my first husband
coming in late from the dock
stinking of fish

he died leaping from the deck
onto a pile of cement blocks
missing the boat entirely

please, don't be like my second husband
enchanting my guts with a sexual sauce
and my brain with a bafflement of words

he died in a room on the coast
through a hole in the floor
mistaking the way out for the way in

bye-bye love you love you love you

lilikoi glowing like the sun
on an old tree in this abandoned orchard
a wild golden plunder

you are born again and again
crusty on the outside and hard
but open, soft and succulent

dripping sweet into my mouth
head, heart and limbs then let me go
bye-bye love you love you love you.

Nightscapes

Border Town

My dress is white
no shoes no pack
through the yard out back
into the barn weak-kneed
under rows of bats
tight in the rafters

I am making a run for it
crossing over
haunted by you forgetting me
and your unsavory types:
the envious, elusive, unpitying,
timber-faced hangers-on

crossing over
into morning light
marking the silvery remains
of touch
places I knew

the handiwork color and line
hooks and hinges
that grace this shrine
the way in
and the way out.

The Bride in the Lime Pit

Hidden by a scraggle
of weed berry bush
a bride lay floating
face down in a slurry lime pit,
her dress confessed to a sensuous event
hands yet tender and wet
wide open for joy

she was missing
there had been a search
the solemn pit man had no words
but splashed an X in green
on an old dark door
where he'd last seen
her walk through

sky hissing
thick with skreaking gull
shuddered to a slow lament:
I was a silly girl
I slipped and fell
love is hell
she whined over summer humming
petticoat lifted
toe snaking
bit by bit to the pit

fairy flotsam
light as white lily
tethered by green filament
to sweet mud
beetle, mint, soul-sickness sick
skittlebug catamarans
cocks-foot and quaking-grass
into the fine liqueur
she slipped
and sank

the halfskip
turned from childish things
and love fell through his veins to his shoes
n-o-o-o-o-o-o-o-o
n-o-o-o-o-o-o-o-o
like a weary bird of passage
from the box of heaven
to frozen ground.

This Way and That

One sun-dappled Saturday Mike came back
his SPAD XIII chugging good to land in the pasture
displacing grasshoppers and biting flies we ran to greet him
there by the funny little house built like a steeple
and kept unlocked for years our hideout with Mike away over
poles north and south and equator trade winds pulling this way
and that on a mission no doubt urgent spy potential to death
by torture.

in a dusty patch the mongrel pup stops scratching and stares
door of the SPAD opening duffel bag and briefcase thrown down
then Mike flopping deep into the old sofa outside crossing his fingers
sighs we hold back.

salsify the drifter
everything goes and returns different some get so small
losing physical bodies like pinpricks in water still and deep
some get bigger cartwheeling from life to death and back in
bloom again on God's third day sustenance and pleasure
objects fly up from childhood go missing that is their charm
to walk raffish wolffia and dandelion away and away to
life with no small craft warning.

Station Café

It happens this way: descent
of cheek to cool linen and
last lazy image of day
eyes draw in and sink
like whisky
to gut from gullet
hot slow tumble down
to blank

crow on a wire gnawing on a chicken bone
turns off like a two-second switch and back
as a shimmery jig-jag stack of coops
a city of bee boxes
or a postcard from the Eastern Bloc

itty bitty bottles of Parisien perfume
scattered on an old maid's vanity
like skipping stones in a dusty courtyard
miles from the sea

looking for a place to pee
the ladies from Minsk (or is it Gdansk) bustle in
waiting for the two-ten to Panyshi (or is it Vertniki)
flowery bedrolls and parcels string-tied for supper
they squat with embroidered headscarves
and voluminous skirts

in the ladies washroom
iridescent cabinet of wonder
tiny chipped tiles and enamel
oily with age and skin and smell
a whistle screams and fades
the attendant sits quietly by
holding a basket of white hand towels.

Special Collections

belly in hot beach sand
evenings lit by fireflies
shelf

father's hard act to follow
the brother who stuttered
shelf

mother's red hair
grandmother's thimble

lost boys
lost boys I loved
shelf

freeways, bad teeth
farm work

guru train to Patna
two months no meat
shelf

thought I would die
I didn't die
shelf

silvery lagoon
chalky sky to the east
above white mountain

hockey clicks and smacks
last play of day
sundown

black silhouette
fading into fire
let go of daylight

let it go.

Love and Pain

Terminal Moraine

If the brown crust
clinging to the corners
of your mouth
marks you a messy man,
the rusty thumb and first finger
forecast danger
code blue
blood in the gutters

Still the sly tongue
poking between your teeth
scours the rim
like a kittycat
content to sit
with its humans

I am your human
but I don't know it yet
the crust in the corners
has made off with my head
and that tongue the licky tongue
well we've only just met

Some say you were a wild thing
and crazy after that
when you read your poems
you are passionate
about men in hotel rooms
alone longing for love,

about the butchery in Darfur
you become weak
heat enters your brain and bowel
and exits your heart
leaving a husk of sang-song twitter
and blue slag

You've been warned
be careful who you love
you aren't careful
aching for my naked shoulders,
I blush reading this
in a letter
alone by the mailbox
and wonder
how would it be to kiss a dragonfish
scabrous cloak, delicate handwings
and eye of octopi

how can one be so hot and so prudish at the same time?

I dream you come to visit:
there's a carton of orange juice
and milk for my tea on the counter
I wash your arms
first the left, then the right
and you roll happily
like a great whale
in a small tub
of deep blue sea

The way it hung together:
two terranes
sun from the east
sun from the west
best clothes in God's closet
the bar, the birthday,
the organ, three pieces of suit
clanging and banging
down the chute,
crumbs to the prayer house.

Writer whose work still moves me to tears

Midnight like smeared mascara over the industrial zone salt air and cagey inhibition our first real date I am driving you home to a pay by the week hotel for pensioners and night owls with sketchy backgrounds dark silhouettes of factories loom and we fly the road as quiet as a solitary life you are peeking at my face in the rear-view mirror and I turn to say good-bye thanks for the movie thanks for everything I'll see you yeah we kiss one time, twice softly you are standing in the shadow of the doorway as I step on the gas back to town shaky and popping like an old beater washed and waxed and started up for the first time in years.

Thrill

When I remember
our evening on the big bed
my heart opens and swallows my desk
all the papers, pencils, brushes, water glass
and the book on Carolingian painting
only light remains and heat and thrill
through the little red door scrolled with gold
and labeled Miss, Girl, Lady, Ma
River of Woe, Boiler of Cabbages,

you find me
and I recognize you.

Aching in the Lowlands

In an old boarding-house in Leuven
too cold for writing
without an overcoat
or a hot drink
too cold to walk to loo
must pee in sink.

Madame D'Hoogue
cooks chicken livers for her cat
in cotton stockings
a British soldier brought her chocolate
after the bombs
of La-Roche-en-Ardenne
leaving behind a daughter with dark hair
and a pleasant disposition.

Madame is mostly frozen
except on Sundays
she walks in sensible shoes
to the little Flemish church
where Jesus Christus
is writhing in pain by candlelight
wooden flesh still warm and bleeding.

she feels something
she feels better.

I Saw Two Crows

In a dried-up parking lot
gravelly with weeds

I saw two crows talking
quietly
by the hurricane fence

I stopped in my tracks
Forgot I was human
Or that they were crows

I knew what this was
at least it seemed familiar
relationship trouble

the male seemed flustered
had something to say to his girl
in crow talk

but could only hop about
swoop in close
and muss with her feathers

clack his beak to her beak

in yawps
was he whispering?
pleading?
sharing food?

I thought birds were flighty
took off in a rush to sky up
away from giants with glinty eyes
and little bags of crumbs

I Saw Two Crows

but these just stood there
in this spot
he upset

she putting up with it
the beak talk, the nudge, the worm
and then she did it

what I have never in my life been able to do
when shoved by a lover with bells on his toes
when facing down stares of passion
sharing the hated worm,

Walk away.

Travail

We are three
almost four
my belly a cradle
since last November
our house is tiny
a chicken coop once
a crazy quilt now
of wood and windows
under the great fir

it's late summer
hills beyond Elk Creek
are trembling
as I make my way
past the last of the leeks
and pole beans
to the fields behind
wet and green in winter
under endless rain
a patchwork now
of dry scrub
and wizened plum trees

I'm walking out
Mistress of Barred Rocks
and Banty Hens
Caretaker of Corn Cobs
and Wood Pile
transported by the scent
of September
mint, lavender, rotting apple
and the sounds
buzzing, flitting
whistling, clicking

Travail

I'm walking out to the bushes
along the cow path
in a straw hat with a bucket
because it's time
blackberry canes swing low
under heavy loads
a dangerous opulence
bursting sweet juice
for pillage

the wooden plank
is still there
askew in the bramble
my walkway to the biggest
and the brightest
I bend to push it deeper
when the scream and dive
of a red-tailed hawk
ignites the thicket
blue jays take off
catcalling indignation
and I, shaken
ungainly on wobbly wood
drop like a sparrow
into the Valley of the Shadow
strong-armed by canes
armed with tiny daggers
sweet black berry blood
on lips knees fingertips

stunned
under vast sky
my belly hard
tangled in vines and dirt
no one will find me
"O mighty One!
who is like You
who sustains the living
with loving kindness
supports the falling
releases the bound
and causes deliverance
to spring forth
through danger"

late afternoon is still
but for whispers of reproach
from a grandmother
and a maiden aunt
back in the city
"we told you so
why did you go
you're not from there"

I walk slowly carefully
along the cow path
small but mighty
hunter gatherer
back to the great fir
swaddled in softening sun
blood beating to grow
each cell rushing
to glorious completion

Travail

evening preparation
for three nearly four:
supper on the hotplate
teapot on the Franklin
door closed for now
to the fields behind.

Shipwreck and Resurrection

[When I was crazy]

When I was crazy
to find what was wrong
I locked my eyes on winter
tracks across the snow
receding back of small circling bird

I finally quit looking
couldn't find a mistake
despite the low sky.

Seward First Winter

On Christmas Eve
Pastor Ben tells it like it is
says he's gonna sing
and he is nervous
exclaiming over and over
to us the hopeful
you wanna make it happen
you gotta sing
sing out
sing your guts out
and he does finally
The First Noel a cappella
shaky to start then strong
really strong
I get it
and bundle out alone
down Fourth to the bay
earthly cold and animal still
to the other clamorous congregation
of aching hearts that sing
"Baby you make me feel"
steeped in holy wine, beer
and peanuts

the night ticking away
to beautiful Christmas.

Shoe slick town by a bay
Resurrection they say
I fear even now
the wall of water
could come any day
carry me past bars, churches
and knick-knack shops
am I the only one waiting
even in dream time
for the sea to slip
mountain to crack
for the siren blast
leave now get in the car
don't forget the kit:
a set of clothes, snacks
the wind-up radio, flashlight and list
of emergency contacts,
or just run
brain singing heart singing
bones singing
as Fourth Avenue slips shakes
grinds its gears
and the sea rises crescendo
of black water and rock
then sleeps

the night ticking away
to beautiful Christmas.

Living after Winter

The Umpqua River rose up
in seventy-four
creeping through the trees
silent under a strange sky
waxy yellow

Highway 138 to Sutherlin
the Volvo growling
like an old dog
Ta Ta Tenne
falling to the left

earth breathes
through a delicate membrane
exhales at night
a scent of belonging
baby I love to touch your skin

Collapse of ice to water
slow crack of ice in spring
ode to living after winter
to busting out streetlamps
in favor of light.

The Boys Outside

are downtown
staring at sidewalks
dragging pit bulls on rope
scrounging for cigarettes
stomachs aching teeth aching
flipping me the bird

boys outside are
wiry under entryways
rolling their own with cool hands
tattoos of exploding skulls and tears
one for each kill they say

it's a sad sight
like crows pecking
at the remnants of a happy meal
when they're almost done
they make a mournful sound

I think about their mothers
leaving work in two degrees
of smoky stillness
sharp intakes of icy breath
through parking lots frozen black

go back
fill the train with wigs in trunks
stack the tent poles high
and wind the Big Top round with straps
go back to the villages
the land and the light.

White Frozen Postcard

All summer long
geese gorge on pondweed
and eelgrass
they waddle about imperiously
bugling like bike horns
and nudge the goslings
into dark fragrant waters.

They are tying up loose ends
and when the flaming sun
sinks into the chilly sea
they play follow the leader
in loopy strands over cove and bay
far from this white frozen postcard.

All summer
earthworms feast underground
on decaying roots and leaves
working and working their way
through hard dirt, pink and unclothed
hauling their harvest to the burrow
where they swallow only the softest bits
and when it rains they set sail upwards
dashing swashbucklers
devotees of the Barge Pilots Manifesto
who navigate the sidewalks
like the canals of Europe.

All summer long
I am walking in my sleep
through hot days of abundance
washed up blown about or stuck
like a pebble in the road
no dip in temperature ripening of berries
impending rain morning frost or twitch of innards
will make me go.

Oh, to know your job
when to leave when to return
open or shut as the light dictates:
sun going – put on sweater mulch perennials head south
sun coming - head north take off sweater plant seeds.

Clan of Stone banish me!
I wish to change my ways.

In Spring

In spring
we lose our reason
quietly waiting
for morning birds
to skip a beat
it's a one-in-five shot
by the window
from the bed
still warm

hwui - hwui
hwui - hwui
hwui -

sunlight cracks
through a watery veil
buds mill about
like gawky debutantes
clutching scented letters
of introduction
and we laugh

Mother of all creation
who made thee
miss a beat
thanks for this moment
of imperfect happiness.

How and Why

Levee

Late June sky dims quick in New Orleans
distant rumbling gets loud and louder
fragrant falling curtain soaks me to the skin
as I run for the car you're sullen
and mercurial as the clouds

This is what you saw:
red x on door dead cat inside dead woman inside
floaters and fire ants shotgun on Danziger Bridge
cockroach clinging to raft of moldy lunch meat
deer head thrown from freezer into river of sewage

My last morning you bring breakfast to the hotel
quiche Lorraine and a berry tart
from Zarin's old place in the Quarter
you say sorry I've behaved badly
something is making me crazy

Once there was Zarin's black hair furry brow
a glorious house of ghosts Modigliani girlfriend
muggy night spent listening to the best guitar leads of all time
voodoo candles placed carefully under the stairs

Bony warm raggedy son
I think you are holding your breath
inching the door shut
waiting for the next levee to break.

Death of the Fish Lizard

Falling into grass Sacha screams then jumps to make me laugh
a birdie in the bush she spied it yesterday and wants to be one
is one, crouched and keening on the sidewalk
for her sippy cup

she's here with me, Grandmother
her skin like beach stone clean and sweet
we sleep as the mud oozes covering dishes and roses
roaring pounding then quiet over hills and ancient sea
Ghizou Province ninety million years ago
ichthyosaur and baby stilled forever swimming in dreamtime

In the field there is a dead cow on the fence
calf hanging behind draped like wet silk
stopped by old wood and a crazy birth dance
I imagine screams and shudder to think that could be me
my animal life to death so quick and necessarily painful,
I bend to pick up the cup for Sacha.

Why Children

To have children is to carry a great stone
tenderly without a horse

swallow a storm
be very tired in dusty houses

yet my waif in a dirty nightgown
restless during the long night

banishes quick the veil
the black over heart and brain

shoves it down to subterranean puddles
where the case of rage lies hidden

to have children is to know hard love
as a trick of the trail.

Slick

black gunk swoops in
over New Orleans
like an assassin in a nursery
gullets freeze
and the young give up the ghost
before hatching.

nightmares are on the rise
children go to bed
dreaming of drowning
in black pools of oil
stinking un-washable
summer camp is canceled.

save the quarters
for animal rescue
save the quarters
for wetlands restoration
swing and sway
and pray for pollywogs
scorched from the inside out.

raise up the second line
for wading birds and sea turtles
tossed into the Valley
of the Shadow of Death
burning like cucarachas
on broken pavement
and spill
into jazz
when blood and bones
are not enough.

Son I wish

Son I wish I could see you
for you remind me
of what it feels like
to be empty
and full
at the same time.
you have a knack
for appearing to me
in dreams
of misplaced children
or unnamed villages.
each day I am
without you I am closer
to myself and I'm happy.
I know I will love your new girl.

Son I wish I could see you
fly out of that shitty town
after twenty years.
I never loved the new girl
though I loved
that you loved.
run away with your pets
and sacred guitar
of the one-eyed jack
glued on by Marty.
abandon the struggle.
there's no shame
in being alone.

Love you forever, lady who gave me life

This morning's note
amazes me warms me
I'm back to that movie
in soft focus
little fingers as pink pearls
buttery stars or field mice
nights breathing
mother be there always

your best friends are dead now:
Roo on Goa worshipped beauty
he fell thirty feet washing windows
then hung himself
an unglamorous exit
for a glamorous man
Marty cool street guy
hanging with the homies
down to 90 pounds
hated the candy bars
you brought to his bedside
and Jesse "drinking salty margaritas
with Fernando" on Monday
teaching the art of blowjobs on Tuesday
slitting his throat Wednesday,
sidekicks who rushed you to manhood

your note this morning makes me sweat
remembering
that dump truck rollover
the little fingers like pink pearls
forty years tracking
a refrain of hurt
sidekicks who pushed you to manhood

a new movie now
in color rewritten recast:
a woman from Irkutsk
nine lives
many blessings
dumb luck
and the DNA
of those who marched into the sea
aiming for Holy Land.

History Lessons

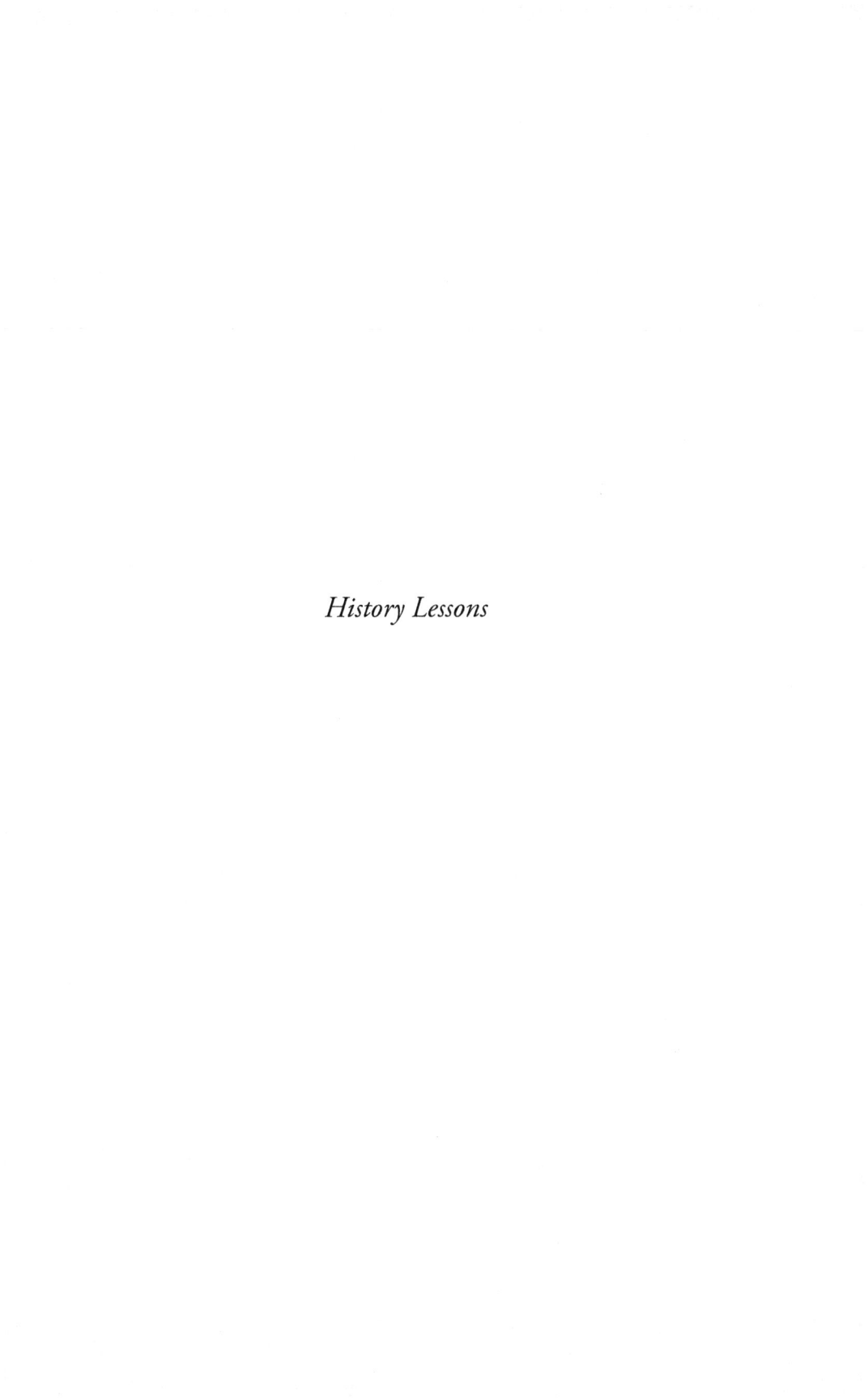

My Alphabet Begins with Y

"You're a twig in the wind"
shuffling along the sidewalk
near the gardens
it's almost winter the starlings jittery
and the twig that flies up and falls
comes from something bigger
returns to something bigger

"It's you, it's all you"
words from Kikas are honey to my heart
echo those rooms
where squatters cast
their silks and papers and pots
each nook a voice, a privacy, a declaration
of animal life absolute

"Be a householder," says Teacher
At his lotus feet I cry
I am promised to someone
But want to stay here under immense sky
The sadhus in the park
The swiftly flowing river
And the temple dancers from Germany

"Nothing is new under the sun"
yet I am planted and sprouting
in luminous air
I am elemental the earth the trees
money in the jar
I catch the night train back
to see a man who can say why.

Playhouse in a Vacant Lot

To all the beloveds in this hut
I am indebted
you pet and pinch and drift along
this world made of paper
this map of kin where the names have changed.

I crawl on my knees with provisions:
a piece of soap a bowl a spoon
eat cereal from wheat
and think of the old woman in the morning
her hair uncombed and teeth in the glass
she cries "my life has always been miserable!"

I am working my fingers
scorched bone, bitter herb, the kiddush cup
rubbing my skin with fat and felting the roof
with rags from the bottom drawer.

I touch my ear to the ground
the earth is breathing stories
of the dead from Kovno to Poughkeepsie
and of the living who bury fish
under the rose bushes in spring.

One and Only Love

On an icy pond at twelve
I skated solo like Amelia
a crummy old pond
where weeds and stones
would trip my tender en pointe
twirling giddy

pond at the end of the street
first home away from home
the frozen woodsmoke smell
as tasty as Grandma's cooking
as personal as a hiding place
behind the curtains

I couldn't wait to get back there
day after bone-chilling day
and perform the old standards
arabesque east of the sun
spinning my one and only love
slow glide tenderly.

A Boy with Lizard Eyes

A boy with lizard eyes
calls my name through picket fence
and hyacinth
to snake among the wilder weeds
as alive to me as the no-name god
to cousins riding horseback
over frozen ground.

Heat from the sand holds me
here my sensuous playhouse hot
and heart beating fast I slither
on belly and dig in with toes
longing to race the wind to beat the wind
and dance the crazy one god two-step
laugh at His no-name.

I see myself in grandfather's slippers woven threads
I see myself Yecutieleh
yud-koof-vav-tav-alef-lamed-hey
your name is, as you know, from the Hebrew
"God will nourish."

In Ostende

we touch in the hayloft
your trembling shoulders facing mine
and anxious eyes like a loose screen door rattling,

low clouds rumble in wet
gusting chilly through barn straw and overcoat
squawking gulls dive-bomb white caps
North Sea blitzkrieg,

I behold the conquering hordes
crushing the thorny forests of Flanders
the perfect loam from sand and clay
for spurry and colza, hops and peas,

the work-horse three years fifteen hands
and mothers their red hair wild
like the crazy defiance of barnyard geese,

rain is hissing down on cobbled streets
on to the roofs of trams
that pass by places of faded wallpaper,
surly bars and silent cathedrals,

the suspicious are waiting to be made new
waiting for forgiveness and power
with rat-a-tat hearts.

Opera

Act One:

She mesmerizes in lantern light   clicking down the hallway in pink plastic pumps

Stops   tosses hair with a flourish, fixes me with a pout

and a quavering voice

am I gonna die?

well   leaves at the end fall to the ground

I don't think it hurts much

she collapses on the carpet   I'm dead Grandma   wanna be dead with me?

I decline

say no to the March of Time

the plants and animals playing musical chairs

sludge burning to diamonds

Jurassic Triassic Permian so on

It's a violent story

"…and the meteorite fell, obliterating droves of earth dwellers and their pet dinos"

Yeah, I don't think it hurt much.

Two:

The father stacks the books where the daughter can just reach them

bodies dumped in pits   piles of shoes   skinny legs and shrunken genitals

people with eyes and knees and grandmothers

beating other people to death, hating them, breaking them into rags and rubbish

At night she dreams of the daddy longlegs

a damp stain marks the spot where it clung for two weeks

partly crushed by a stack of phone books

she awakens to the scurry and chatter of wings and beaks

crying like twigs in a hurricane.

Three:

Antidote to fear
of closed spaces, horrible faces
open fields, great heights,
bees, monsters, raccoons, robots,
and Black Hairy Tongue:
coax paper into cracks
sigh a winter breath
touch skin to late night fire
pad walls with coats of the Old Ones
line tins with fur
work and wait like spider.

Dancing from Warsaw to Vilna in Black and White

Ada Acker slid through my childhood
two-wheeling on icy cobblestone
her ghost strolls through my night
sipping Polish cocoa, breathing passwords to all the little locks

In 1943, she outran the killers
the rooms and the gardens pulled her tightly as if to say "she's one of us"
when blinking at the sea from the cliff
she thought of the chipped blue teacup left on the bench and leaped

I return to Warsaw
there she moans as wind aching through walls
calling to the other broken vessels of first light
vanished to the center of my skull behind the One Great Eye

The girl drags a trunk to the train
a flight of words, whispers in the station café
he touches her breast through wool she gives him her eyes
it's rainy but the butter sweet,

One hundred kilometers underground, red-hot magma flows
loosening cobblestones by the booksellers' market
breaking the walls that border the park
vows are always made at times like these

The war began when I was five
I had barely learned to talk in rhyme
"we are here; we are here" was a ditty from those days sung with pistol in
  hand
and Marysia, the nightingale of Leszno Street, shone like a meteor with
  special light

I'm herding tired people now to the elevator
to a room where they'll be safe
then I drop into a hole and am no more
all those I knew have passed with a shrug to the center of my skull
behind the One Great Eye.

"We are here; we are here" is a reference to "Zog nit keynmol az du geyst dem letstn veg" (Never say that you are walking the final road), also known as "The Partisans' Song," is perhaps the best-known of the Yiddish songs created during the Holocaust. It was written in 1943 by the young Vilna poet Hirsh Glik and based on a pre-existing melody by the Soviet-Jewish composer Dimitri Pokrass. Inspired by the news of the Warsaw ghetto uprising, the song was adopted as the official anthem of the Vilna partisans.

Acknowledgments

I would like to thank Mike Burwell, Sandra Kleven, Hugo House, 10 Poets, Poetry Parley, Steven Jay Bernstein, Martin Marriott and Red Sky Poetry Theatre for their inspiration and guidance.

I want to thank my family for their unconditional support.
I love you so much.
In blessed memory, I honor my parents Lillian and Norman Moonitz, my paternal grandparents Ethel and Louis Moonitz, my maternal grandparents Jacob and Yetta Birn, my great-aunts Sonya Moonitz, Rena Kaplin, and Betty Krieger, my uncles David Moonitz, Charles Eisenberg, and Harry Mergel, and my aunts Frieda Taplin, Mildred Mergel, and Molly Eisenberg. You provided me with a childhood of affection, wonder and adventure, as well as awakened in me an interest in my cultural, ethnic and religious identity.

Many thanks to Carly Egli for her creative eye,
design skills and great work ethic.

A special thanks to Brenda Hill and James Keele

Previously Published:

Cirque: "Existential Texas," "Afterwards," "Lilikoi," "Bordertown," "Aching in the Lowlands," "A Boy with Lizard Eyes," "In Ostende," "Dancing from Warsaw to Vilna in Black and White," "Son I Wish," "The Boys from Outside," and "My Man"

Drash: Northwest Mosaic: "Dancing from Warsaw to Vilna in Black and White"

About the Author

Leslie Fried was born in Tel Aviv, Israel and came to New York at the age of six. Her parents' families came from Poland and Lithuania and ultimately settled in Brooklyn. She turned to poetry after thirty years as a scenic artist in theater and film, and a muralist working in paint and plaster. Her writing reflects her love of imagery as a means for addressing difficult subjects. In this, her first book, she draws on the themes of death, love, family and history to weave her emotional tapestries. Ms. Fried is Curator of the Alaska Jewish Museum in Anchorage. She has two sons, Daniel and Julien, and a granddaughter Sacha.

About Cirque Press

Cirque Press grew out of *Cirque*, a literary journal established in 2009 by Michael Burwell, as a vehicle for the publication of writers and artists of the North Pacific Rim. This region is broadly defined as reaching north from Oregon to the Yukon Territory and south through Alaska to Hawaii – and west to the Russian Far East. Sandra Kleven joined *Cirque* in 2012 working as a partner with Burwell.

Our contributors are widely published in an array of journals. Their writing is significant. It is personal. It is strong. It draws on these regions in ways that add to the culture of places.

We felt that the works of individual writers could be lost if it were to remain scattered across the literary landscape. Therefore, we established a press to collect these writing efforts. Cirque Press seeks to gather the work of our contributors into book form where it can be experienced coherently as statement, observation, and artistry.

Sandra Kleven – Michael Burwell, publishers and editors
www.cirquejournal.com

Books from Cirque Press

Apportioning the Light by Karen Tschannen (2018)

The Lure of Impermanence by Carey Taylor (2018)

Echolocation by Kristin Berger (2018)

Like Painted Kites & Collected Works by Clifton Bates (2019)

Athabaskan Fractal: Poems of the Far North by Karla Linn Merrifield (2019)

Holy Ghost Town by Tim Sherry (2019)

Drunk on Love: Twelve Stories to Savor Responsibly by Kerry Dean Feldman (2019)

Wide Open Eyes: Surfacing from Vietnam by Paul Kirk Haeder (2020)

Silty Water People by Vivian Faith Prescott (2020)

Life Revised by Leah Stenson (2020)

Oasis Earth: Planet in Peril by Rick Steiner (2020)

The Way to Gaamaak Cove by Doug Pope (2020)

Loggers Don't Make Love by Dave Rowan (2020)

The Dream That Is Childhood by Sandra Wassilie (2020)

Seward Soundboard by Sean Ulman (2020)

The Fox Boy by Gretchen Brinck (2021)

Lily Is Leaving: Poems by Leslie A. Fried (2021)

CIRCLES Imprint

Lullaby for Baby Abe by Ann Chandonnet (2021)

More Praise for *Lily is Leaving: Poems by Leslie A. Fried*

Leslie Fried is an archeologist of the soul, digging through the fractured histories of ancestors, and her own past with parents, lovers and sons, to describe the forces that mold our characters and haunt our dreams. She uses her acute powers of observation, and vivid images and metaphors, to relate both the depths of trauma and the heights of delight. She is particularly adept at revealing the deceitfulness we all use to bind others to ourselves and to make sense of our histories. In Leslie's poetic world, time is not linear, love covers a multitude of pains and disappointments, and grace is still possible.

—Tonja Woelber, author of the poetry collections *Glacier Blue* (2016) and *Tundra Songs* (2017)

In her debut collection, *Lily is Leaving*, Leslie Fried writes "on the train my shadow is my letter of introduction." These poems are marked by their sensitivity to lives in transit, lives that need to journey in order to prosper, and, at times, to simply survive. When the speaker finds shelter, it's often outwardly flimsy - "our house is tiny / a chicken coop once / a crazy quilt now / of wood and windows / under the great fir" - but Fried vividly shows us how familial bonds deepen and intimacy flourishes in such idiosyncratic spaces. Indeed, the author delights in all invitations, large or small, that the world extends. And her poems make us at home in that world, as if we, too, are invited to live fully. For instance, she accepts an "Invitation to an Intimate Dinner Room 43, Airport Way South," and dines at "a small square table / covered in butcher paper / folded and taped" an experience that could have passed her by, had she let it. This is a narrator who takes her knocks at times because, fundamentally, she's in cahoots with abundance. When Fried tells us "I am planted and sprouting / in luminous air," we believe her.

—Deborah Woodard, author of *Plato's Bad Horse* (2006), *Borrowed Tales* (2012), and *No Finis: Triangle Testimonies, 1911* (2018)

Leslie Fried's debut collection offers an elegance in language illuminating carefully crafted poems that invite me to read and re-read lines, verses, and whole poems as I discover fresh angles, peepholes and circumstances to experience: ardor, family, history, loss, intimacy, death; to. . .know hard love as a trick of the trail. . .Here is a lively edginess of surprises along with Fried's descriptions of place, each so vivid you might remember them later as if you had physically been there.

It is a gift. Her gift is extended by her own illustrations. Delicate and impish special treats. For my own pleasure, I read the poems aloud to myself, and discover more heart, more about being alive as. . .the earth is breathing stories. . .

>—Carol Levin, author of *Stunned by Velocity* (2012), *Confident Music Would Fly Us to Paradise* (2014), and *An Undercurrent of Jitters* (2018)

Lucky poets get to dream up, assemble and order one life, and make of it what they will. But then some find themselves chained to livings full of extremes, of impossible aspirations, cravings and doubts that will not leave them be, no matter what. In her new book, Leslie Fried's livings seem made up of restless migrations, east to west and back, seasonal north to south and back. There are choices made to be deeply lived, rewarded with beauty, ruptured innocence, terror and unbounded love in her shared lives. And in her commemoration of losses, of which her mother Lily is but the most recent, the poet finds herself nudging into port like a small boat, into what she calls "the business of living," unfinished as ever, with its elegies, greetings and partings, with its ashes fed to the wind from the heights. Her poems are plain-spoken and alive. We feel them beating in our throats.

>—Paul Hunter, author of *Come the Harvest* (2008), *Stubble Field* (2012), and *Clownery: In lieu of a life spent in harness* (2017)

Leslie Fried - daughter, lover, mother, grandmother - welcomes readers to join "all the beloveds in this hut," an expansive and deeply human book that spans geographies and generations. Propelled by memory and witness, wish and rue, and logics both lyric and narrative, the poet sets her metronome to a "universe pumping slow time," quickening and refracting its rhythms and shadows till it's possible to sense how "the earth is breathing stories."

>—Jeremy Pataky, author of *Overwinter*

Made in the USA
Coppell, TX
13 June 2023